D1175545

Our Amazing States™

Georgia

The Peach State

Marcia Amidon Lusted

PowerKiDS press.
New York

For my son Tom, with love

Published in 2010 by The Rosen Publishing Group, Inc.
29 East 21st Street, New York, NY 10010

First Edition

Editor: Nicole Pristash
Book Design: Greg Tucker
Photo Researcher: Jessica Gerweck

Photo Credits: Cover Walter Bibikow/Getty Images; pp. 5, 22 (tree), 22 (insect), 22 (flag), 22 (bird), 22 (flower) Shutterstock.com; p. 7 © Corbis; pp. 9, 22 (Martin Luther King Jr.) Hulton Archive/Getty Images; p. 11 © James Randklev/Corbis; p. 13 David Muench/Getty Images; p. 15 Inga Spence/Getty Images; p. 17 © Bachmann/age fotostock; p. 19 Robert F. Sisson/Getty Images; p. 22 (Jimmy Carter) AFP/Getty Images; p. 22 (Dakota Fanning) Stephen Lovekin/Getty Images.

Library of Congress Cataloging-in-Publication Data

Lusted, Marcia Amidon.
Georgia : the Peach State / Marcia Amidon Lusted. — 1st ed.
p. cm. — (Our amazing states)
Includes index.
ISBN 978-1-4042-8149-3 (library binding) — ISBN 978-1-4358-3376-0 (pbk.) —
ISBN 978-1-4358-3377-7 (6-pack)
1. Georgia—Juvenile literature. I. Title.
F286.3.L87 2010
975.8—dc22
2009008686

Manufactured in the United States of America

Contents

Soda, Swamps, and Civil Rights

There is a state that is home to the Coca-Cola company, has **swamps** filled with alligators, and is famous for growing tasty peaches. Which state has all these things and more? Georgia does!

Georgia is found in the southern part of the United States, just north of Florida. Alabama lies to the west, and South Carolina is north of the state. Georgia's east side touches the Atlantic Ocean.

Throughout history, many important events have taken place in Georgia. **Civil War** battles were fought throughout the state. Dr. Martin Luther King Jr. helped start the **civil rights movement** from Georgia, too.

This is the fountain inside Forsyth Park, in Savannah. Savannah, a city on Georgia's east coast, is known for its beautiful parks, buildings, and rich history.

Colonies and Cotton

The first European to **explore** the area that is now Georgia was the Spanish explorer Hernando de Soto in 1540. Then, the English founded a colony there in 1732. It was named Georgia after King George II. It became the last of the 13 British colonies in America.

After the **American Revolution**, Georgia became the fourth state to join the new United States of America. People bought land there and began to grow cotton, which became the most common crop grown in the South. By the time of the Civil War, farmers in Georgia needed **slaves** to work in their fields and harvest, or gather, their cotton. These farmers depended on their slaves.

This image shows slaves picking cotton on a Georgia farm. Slavery was a common practice in the South during the nineteenth century.

War in Georgia

Abraham Lincoln was elected president in 1860. At this time, many Southerners felt that they were taxed unfairly. They wanted each state to make its own decisions. Many Northerners wanted Lincoln to end slavery. Lincoln wanted to keep the Union, or country, together. Some Southern states, such as Georgia, **seceded**. They formed the **Confederate** States of America and went to war against the Union in 1861. This was the Civil War.

Several important battles took place in Georgia. The battle of Chickamauga was one of the bloodiest. At Kennesaw Mountain, the Confederates beat the Union soldiers. The Confederates, though, **surrendered** in 1865, and the war ended. Georgia rejoined the Union in 1870.

The battle of Chickamauga, shown here, took place from September 18 to September 20, 1863. More than 34,000 soldiers went missing, were hurt, or were killed during the battle.

Mountains, Islands, and Heat

Georgia has everything from mountains to plains to islands and rivers. The Blue Ridge Mountains are found in northern Georgia. Midway through the state, there is a flat plain along the coast. The Okefenokee Swamp sits on the border of Florida in southeastern Georgia. You can find the Chattahoochee River flowing along part of the border of Georgia and Alabama. There is also the Savannah River, on the border of Georgia and South Carolina. The state also has a row of **barrier** islands off the coast.

Georgia's weather is uncomfortable in the summer. The temperature can reach more than 100° F (38° C). Winters are cooler, and it sometimes snows in the mountains.

This is St. Catherines Island, one of Georgia's barrier islands. The middle part of the island is used as a place where animals that are in danger of dying out are kept safe.

Georgia Wildlife

Georgia has many interesting animals, such as alligators, wild pigs, wild turkeys, and flying squirrels. Whales and dolphins swim in the ocean off Georgia's coast. Leatherback sea turtles share the water with them. Even armadillos and rattlesnakes can be found in Georgia!

Each area of Georgia has different types of plants. Scrub pine trees grow on the barrier islands. Trees such as bamboo and cypress grow in the swamps of Georgia.

Georgia's state flower is the Cherokee rose. The Cherokee **tribe** helped plant many of these flowers, and they grow all over the state. Cherokee roses are white with large golden yellow centers.

Alligators can be found living in Georgia's swamps. They eat fish, snails, and animals that often come near the water, such as birds.

Peaches and More

Georgia's nickname is the Peach State because peaches are the crop the state is best known for. Farmers grow other crops there, too, such as pecans and peanuts. Farmers in Georgia also raise chickens and cows.

Georgia companies and factories make many goods that are used all over the country. Atlanta is home to the Coca-Cola soft drink company. Coca-Cola is one of the most popular sodas in the world. Other factories in Georgia build fighter jets.

Georgia clay is mined and sent all over the world to make cat litter and paint. Rocks such as granite and limestone are mined and used to build homes and office buildings.

Even though Georgia is not the state that produces the largest number of peaches, Georgia peaches are known for tasting the best.

A Visit to Atlanta

Atlanta, a city in the northern part of the state, became the capital of Georgia in 1868. The city was built near the Chattahoochee River, and more than 500,000 people live there today. The city is known for being Dr. Martin Luther King Jr.'s home. King's group, the Southern Christian Leadership Conference, or SCLC, was based in Atlanta during the civil rights movement of the 1960s. Visitors can see King's grave at the King Center.

Visitors to Atlanta can also explore the World of Coca-Cola or watch whales at the Georgia Aquarium. You can visit the world's largest oil painting, called *The Battle of Atlanta*, at the Atlanta Cyclorama and Civil War Museum in Grant Park.

Here you can see Dr. Martin Luther King Jr.'s grave at the King Center, in Atlanta. More than 600,000 people visit there every year.

Land of the Trembling Earth

One of Georgia's greatest natural sites is the Okefenokee National Wildlife **Refuge**. It is located in southeastern Georgia. The refuge is home to Okefenokee Swamp, the second-largest freshwater swamp in the world. *Okefenokee* means "land of the trembling earth" because the swamp has floating islands of grass and **peat** that shift and move over the water. Okefenokee Refuge is about the size of 300,000 football fields! It has many different kinds of animals living in it, such as alligators, snakes, and snapping turtles. Cypress trees hung with moss tower above the water.

Visitors to Okefenokee can explore the swamp. You can go by boat or walk on trails.

Okefenokee Swamp, shown here, is 38 miles (61 km) long and 25 miles (40 km) wide.

Come to Georgia

Georgia is a great place to visit. You can learn some of Georgia's interesting history at a Civil War battlefield or at the King Center in Atlanta. You can eat some Georgia peaches or watch alligators and snakes in the Okefenokee Swamp. You can also visit Stone Mountain Park, in the town of Stone Mountain. Stone Mountain Park has the world's largest **sculpture** cut right into the mountainside. The sculpture is of Jefferson Davis, Robert E. Lee, and Stonewall Jackson. They are three famous Confederates of the Civil War.

Whether you are a visitor or if you call the state home, Georgia is a special place. There is plenty to do and see!

Glossary

American Revolution (uh-MER-uh-ken reh-vuh-LOO-shun) Battles that soldiers from the colonies fought against Britain for freedom from 1775 to 1783.

barrier (BAR-ee-er) Something that blocks something else from passing.

civil rights movement (SIH-vul RYTS MOOV-mint) People and groups working together to win freedom and equality for all.

Civil War (SIH-vul WOR) The war fought between the Northern and the Southern states of America from 1861 to 1865.

Confederate (kun-FEH-duh-ret) Relating to the group of people who made up the Confederate States of America.

explore (ek-SPLOR) To travel over little-known land.

peat (PEET) Partly rotted plant matter found in some wetlands.

refuge (REH-fyooj) A place that gives shelter or security.

sculpture (SKULP-cher) A figure that is carved, cut, or formed.

seceded (sih-SEED-ed) Withdrew from a group or a country.

slaves (SLAYVZ) People who are "owned" by other people and are forced to work without pay.

surrendered (suh-REN-derd) Gave up.

swamps (SWOMPS) Wetlands with a lot of trees and bushes.

tribe (TRYB) A group of people who share the same way of living, language, and relatives.

Georgia State Symbols

State Tree
Live Oak

State Insect
Honeybee

State Flag

State Bird
Brown Thrasher

State Flower
Cherokee Rose

State Seal

Famous People from Georgia

Jimmy Carter
(1924–)
Born in Plains, GA
U.S. President

Dr. Martin Luther King Jr.
(1929–1968)
Born in Atlanta, GA
Civil Rights Leader

Dakota Fanning
(1994–)
Born in Conyers, GA
Actress

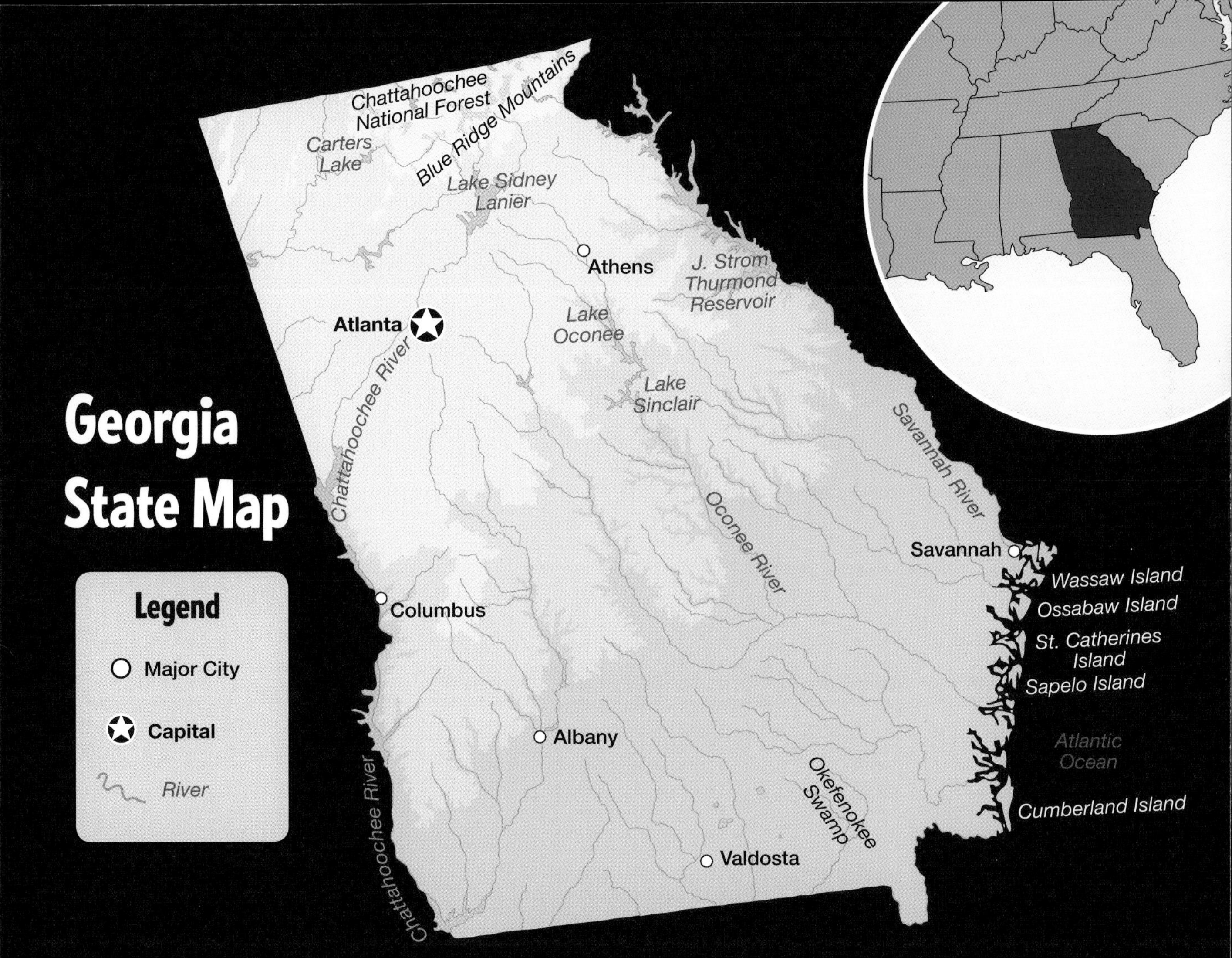

Georgia State Facts

Population: About 8,186,453

Area: 58,910 square miles (152,576 sq km)

Motto: “Wisdom, justice, moderation”

Song: “Georgia on My Mind,” words by Stuart Gorrell, music by Hoagy Carmichael

Index

Web Sites

Due to the changing nature of Internet links, PowerKids Press has developed an online list of Web sites related to the subject of this book. This site is updated regularly. Please use this link to access the list:

www.powerkidslinks.com/amst/ga/